W9-DDX-615

SPRING
RAIN

SPRING RAIN

A GRAPHIC MEMOIR of LOVE, MADNESS, AND REVOLUTIONS

BY ANDY WARNER

ST. MARTIN'S GRIFFIN
NEW YORK

First published by St. Martin's Press,
an imprint of St. Martin's Publishing Group

SPRING RAIN. Copyright ©2020 by Andy Warner.
All rights reserved. Printed in the United States of America.
For information, address St. Martin's Publishing Group,
120 Broadway, New York, NY 10271.

www.stmartins.com

Illustrated by Andy Warner

The Library of Congress Cataloging-in-Publication Data is available upon request.

ISBN 978-1-250-16597-8

Our books may be purchased in bulk for promotional, educational,
or business use. Please contact your local bookseller or the
Macmillan Corporate and Premium Sales Department at
1-800-221-7945, extension 5442, or by email at
MacmillanSpecialMarkets@macmillan.com.

First Edition: January 2020

10 9 8 7 6 5 4 3 2 1

For Beirut:
You are so much more than your political violence or the stories
outsiders tell about you. Please forgive me for telling another.

Welcome to Lebanon.

Shu- ...kran?

I moved to Beirut to study Lebanese literature for a semester in late January of 2005, less than a month after my 21st birthday. My Arabic was terrible.

In the space of three months, the former prime minister was assassinated in a massive car bomb, the government fell, and I lost my mind.

I have a diary from the time that I've used to piece the story back together.

It's hard to reread.

I was young. Everything I felt was intense and meaningful.

I come off like an idiot.

Keeping a diary at all was unusual. I'd had one when I was young, growing up abroad with my family.

CHIK CHIK CHIK

My dad is a marine biologist and we moved from island to island, following his research.

I think my mom wanted us to have a record of the places we lived and travelled.

MOM!! DAD!! WE FOUND A HERMIT CRAB!

After my brother and sister and I went to sleep, my mom would write to us in our own diaries, pretending to be the journal itself.

We'd wake up in the morning to new questions asking us about the day before.

How do you spell hermit crab?

I don't remember when I figured out it was her writing back to me, but by the time I was in middle school, I'd stopped keeping a diary.

what animal did you see at the beach? a hermut crab

going to the bech

I'd started studying Arab literature by chance—a seminar on Abbasid poetry I took my Freshman year introduced me to a world I knew nothing about.

I took more classes.

I was bad at learning the language, but the stories and histories were fascinating and new.

I loved books. Beirut was a city of them.

And in 2005, Beirut was on the up-and-up.

VROOM

Lebanese society is a cosmopolitan mix of 18 officially recognized religious sects ranging from Sunni Muslim to Maronite Christian, Druze to Armenian Apostolic.

That diversity had a heavy price— a 15-year civil war that claimed upwards of a quarter-million lives.

Its scars were etched everywhere in the city.

But that war had ended 15 years before.

Dollars are fine.

The place was buzzing with potential.

5

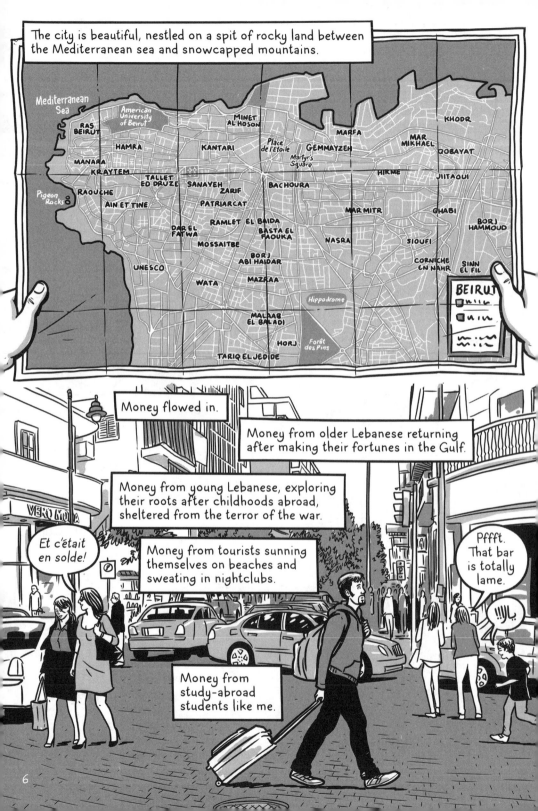

And within that business, the American University of Beirut was a leafy oasis swarming with cats.

My first week in the country sped by. There were a million things to get done before school started. One big one—find a new place to live.

The student I was assigned to be roommates with in the dorms and I hadn't been getting along.

This was worsened by a bout of paranoia that I couldn't shake.

I became convinced that he'd been reading my diary.

I needed to leave, find my own place.
A journalist I'd met on campus told me he might have a lead.
And so the defining pieces of my life in Beirut began to fall into place.
This is Andy.
He's one of the new students.
Hi!
I'm Jason. I'm doing a Ph.D. at the University.
Hey, I'm Sami.
I'm a photographer.
Nice to meet you.
Nice to meet you, too! You're American?
Lebanese-American.
My family lives in Boston.
CAFÉ
Didn't you guys say the apartment next to yours was open?
Andy needs a place to stay.
Yeah, it's still empty, right Sam?
I can get the keys from the landlord. I'll talk to him tonight.
I'll be on campus tomorrow. I can meet you and walk you over.
It's on the other side of Hamra.

12

13

15

It dislodged something deep inside me.

I could feel it with every step, with every drink, rattling around loose.

♪ ♫ ...tics meet the same fate someday, cynical and drun... ♪ ...some... ...laugh, he said yo... immun... ♪ ♫

The first night we met, we were 18 years old, our second semester of college.

She was the lab partner of my friend Christine.

She was funny, smart, easy to talk to.

We got drunk on the vodka my roommate had hidden under his bed and she watched intently as I drew on her arm with a permanent marker.

We were friends for two years, dating other people, smiling at each other when we passed in the quad.

Then, in our Junior year, as late summer turned to fall, we went on a walk together, down by the tracks.

We climbed train cars.

It was early evening, streetlights shone orange, and insects buzzed around us.

She twisted her ankle leaping over a stream behind the grocery store.

We kissed.

The hairs on the back of my neck prickled.

A buzzing worked its way up from the base of my spine to my skull.

Euphoria.

It's even more new. Only three years old, I think.

See, there's construction cranes on that side. It's not even done yet!

This guy named Rafik Hariri is building it. He's, like, the richest man in Lebanon.

Doesn't surprise me. That thing is massive.

I was reading about it all this morning.

Look, when they were digging out the foundation, they found all these ruins from when Beirut was a Roman city.

You've never tried it with a guy, right?

25

26

I guess that explains why this part of the city is called Martyr's Square.

This was the front line in the war, right?

Yeah, I think so. See, look at the bullet holes in the statue.

But they didn't restore it, just left it fucked up.

It sort of feels like a different kind of memorial now.

The cave-like internet café near my apartment, was a tenuous line connecting me to Kathy, far away in Senegal.

I was shit at email.

My diary is filled with adolescent agonizing at being unable to express myself, but I have no record of what we actually wrote to each other.

Webmail - Microsoft Internet Explorer

w Favorites Tools Help

Search Favorites

Address http://webmail.cornell.edu

To   kcg22@cornell.edu

Subject   Re: I miss you

cc

Hi kathy,
I'm sorry I didn't respond, I had to I

Years later, after I began to work on this book, I asked our old university how to access my college account.

I received a curt response: "I regret to inform you that Cornell maintains archives of inactive email accounts for 30 days.

"After that, email from inactive accounts is deleted."

Classes at the University started.

Alone in my apartment at the end of the school day, the power went out.

I bought some candles. To pass the time I started doodling a comic about a strange event I half remembered from my childhood.

We lived in England at the time, in a two-story house with a chestnut tree out front on a dead-end street.

There, in the upstairs bedroom, I briefly developed the power to control my dreams.

I had good memories of England, but adjusting was hard at first.

I was bullied at school for being a foreigner.

Every night, I had nightmares.

Then one night I discovered that if I became aware that I was sleeping, I could pull out of a bad dream.

I would find myself floating in a sea of black, surrounded by a thousand stars.

A million stars.

A billion stars.

By focusing on one, I could force myself into a new dream.

A better dream.

The ability lasted for a week, then was gone as suddenly as I'd acquired it.

I'd been getting back into drawing again, and it felt good. As a child, I drew comics constantly.

I told anyone who'd listen that I was going to be a cartoonist when I grew up.

I stopped when I was a teenager.

So much was changing in my life then that I can't even remember why.

Picking up the practice again gave me a connection to that younger self.

The dream story was a window into the contradictions I still felt from my childhood.

The magic of moving from place to place.

The darkness of finding myself a stranger to my old friends every time we returned to the States.

The following day was Valentine's Day. I was back in the internet café, writing Kathy an email.

I don't remember if it was romantic or apologetic.

Then the world changed.

BOOM

A massive boom roared up from the earth, shaking the concrete walls.

Dust from the particle-board ceiling drifted down like snow.

31

What was that?

My cell phone isn't working.

I don't know!

WEEEEEOOOH!

CD Burning · Printing
Internet Café
& Network Game

WEEEEEOOOH!

WEEEEOOH

Salim!

WEEEEEOOOOOOOH!

WEEEEEOOOH!

What happened?

Was that a bomb?

I don't know! Everybody's freaking out.

I think the cell phone network's down.

I was talking with one of the University guards.

He said it was Rafik Hariri! They tried to kill him.

WEE OOH

WE OOOH

The guy building that giant mosque? Why?

Welcome to Lebanon.

32

35

Hello?

Hey! It's Sunan.

Did you hear those helicopters?

I'm downtown, it's Hariri's funeral.

There's so many people here!

Be right there. I'll get a taxi.

Hariri's body was to arrive at the grand mosque he'd built at noon, but its progress was slowed by the masses surging around it.

People wept.

People fainted.

The coffin, draped with the Lebanese flag, passed so close to us that my extended hand could almost touch it.

Young men climbed the mosque's scaffolding for a better view.

BEEP BEEP

Later, as night fell, cars with loudspeakers strapped to their roofs prowled through the neighborhoods, booming eulogies into the darkness.

BANG! BANG! guh?.

BANG! BANG!

We're going to go take pictures of the blast site and Hariri's grave.

You doing anything important?

Two days after the death of its richest son, Beirut was beautiful.

The sea shone. Hot breezes blew through the streets.

The snow glistened white on the mountains above the city.

Every window on the block was blown out.

CLICK! CLICK

click! click!

Jesus.

Shards of broken glass twinkled in gutters.

CLICK! CLICK!

Buildings were twisted like pretzels.

Cars were strewn about like discarded toys.

Surreality hung heavy. We'd stepped into a shadow world.

We walked back to Martyr's Square.

Hariri's grave was covered with flowers.

Crowds in black filed past.

CLICK!

CLICK! CLICK!

الحقيقة
THE TRUTH

39

The leaders of the opposition called for a nonviolent uprising to drive the Syrian army from Lebanon.

Marches were planned for the 21st of February.

Beirut turned out in force.

CLICK!

Sami brought his camera, and we let ourselves be caught up and pulled along in the crowds.

I could feel a strange electricity.

A collective stirring.

Police watched tensely from the sidewalks.

44

One Sunday, I wrote "I came here to stop going crazy, but it's catching up to me."

Two days later, I recorded that I felt a throbbing pain behind my left eye, like something was gnawing inside my head.

It was awful.

I wanted to rip it out.

45

I'd begun to notice the same few people in the shadowed corners of my vision.

I couldn't shake the feeling that I was being followed.

I saw an older woman with an African gray parrot on her shoulder.

The next day I saw her again.

Then again.

Then again.

In my diary, between entries, I drew images of a man opening his chest to reveal a knotted, teeming mass.

47

It was unsettling.

When I was a teenager, my mom had told me:

Our family had a hist...

My grandmother suffered from bipolar disorder.

She was a sculptor, and the stone bust of a baker named Fred that she carved kept watch near the door to my bedroom growing up.

My mom remembers the stories of her mother's electroshock therapy, and a terrible breakdown when they were living in Mexico.

I have copies of family photos from then. Everyone smiles.

By the time my mom was old enough to be aware, the family had moved to Trinidad, following my grandfather's research on malaria.

Her mother was taking medication.

She was calm.

There are photos of Carnival, and the family's pet monkey, Cheetah.

Years later, after they moved back to Connecticut, my mom's younger sister took that medication from their mother's medicine cabinet and overdosed.

The family believes it was an accident.

My mom found her body.

Her sister's death affected my mom profoundly.

She was her closest family member, her best friend.

My mom buried it.

She found my dad.

They drove to Guatemala in a Volkswagen van. They moved to Panama. It came back out.

She went through therapy. She figured out how to deal with it.

But it stayed with her.

I've never been sure if it was connected, but my mom has always had an irrational fear that she or her children would die by falling, a fear exacerbated by her vertigo.

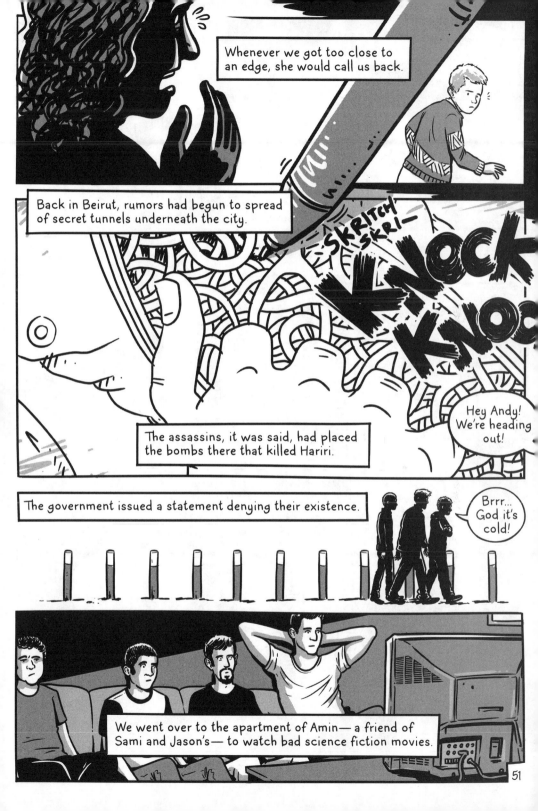

Whenever we got too close to an edge, she would call us back.

Back in Beirut, rumors had begun to spread of secret tunnels underneath the city.

SKRITCH SKRI—

KNOCK KNOC

Hey Andy! We're heading out!

The assassins, it was said, had placed the bombs there that killed Hariri.

The government issued a statement denying their existence.

Brrr... God it's cold!

We went over to the apartment of Amin— a friend of Sami and Jason's— to watch bad science fiction movies.

51

53

The marches continued almost every day.

A protest camp occupied Martyr's Square.

TVs everywhere were tuned to a feed from Parliament, where the pro- and anti-Syrian politicians were having it out with each other.

One night, Salim, Sunan, and I went downtown to eat dinner, but found the streets empty, except for dozens and dozens of soldiers.

An eerie calm had blanketed Beirut.

The following day, the prime minister resigned and dissolved his cabinet.

BEEP! RATATATA!! POW! POW! POW! RATATATA!! BEEP! BEEP! RATATA! POW! POW!

RATATATA!! POW! POW! POW! POW! RATATA! RATATA! POW! POW!

Celebratory gunfire crackled in the cool evening air.

I ran to Sunan's apartment.

BEEP! BEEP! BEEP! BEEP! BEEP! BEEP!

Cars full of young people, shouting and smiling, jammed the city streets.

You were right! The government fell!

I just saw it on TV!

Let's go downtown again!

The tense atmosphere from the day before had vanished.

Soldiers lounged on their barricades, chatting.

As the national mood soared, my own soured.

Kathy's face haunted the crowds around me, vanishing when I looked closer.

Each day, as my mind and the world around me grew increasingly chaotic, I found it more and more difficult to reach out to her.

tap tap tap

I spent my nights drawing feverishly, working to finish the story about dreams.

WHERE THE COYOTES HOWLED AT NIGHT IN THE VACANT LOT NEXT DOOR AND THE OF THROU

skritch skritch

TIL HE GOT A LITTLE TO

I started to cultivate unfamiliar rituals.

The wart I'd torn out began to regrow.

58

I ended the comic with a memory from sixth grade.

The teacher had asked each student to tell a recurring dream.

I told the story of one of the nightmares, before I realized 1 could change them.

I would find myself in the dark, in a hallway.

And something horrible is chasing me.

So I run, not looking back.

But I run slower and slower.

And as my feet become heavy, I know that it will catch me.

And then

after a while

I'd wake up.

59

For a moment, I felt okay.

I was coming to grips with myself, and I was using art to do it.

If I could do it with this story, I could do it with other ones.

An excitement was building.

I was onto something.

It passed.

Holy shit, did you see that guy's gun?

Protesters stayed camped out at Martyr's Square, demanding the withdrawal of all Syrian troops from Lebanese soil and the resignation of Lebanon's pro-Syrian president.

HONK HONK

FREE LEBANON

The nights became loud with sirens and slogans shouted through megaphones.

Helicopters swarmed the skies.

CHOKKA CHOKKA CHOKKA CHOKKA CHOKKA CHOKKA CHOKKA CHOKKA

But the city stayed peaceful.

CHOKKA CHOKKA CHOKKA CHOKKA CHOKKA

Hey, you're a buddy of Sami and Jason's, right?

Jesus!

Sorry, didn't mean to scare you.

I'm not too dangerous. I'm Sara.

Andy.

Nice to meet you, Andy. You smoke hash?

Uh. Yeah, sure.

Thanks.

This is your apartment, right?

Not for long. I'm leaving the country in a week.

Where to?

Back to Canada. Going to see family. It's gotta happen.

Nice. ...Will that be nice?

Eh, somewhat nice.

Pretty strange time to leave, I'd imagine.

All times are strange times.

What's the music playing inside? It's beautiful.

Nick Drake.

I've never heard of him. Did it just come out?

What?

Hahaha! Snort! Andy, this album was released in 1972.

63

He killed himself, actually. Two years after it came out.

Pills.

Lots and lots of pills.

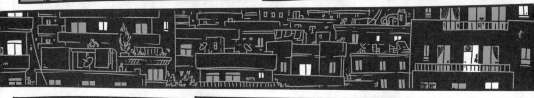

I'll burn you a CD.

flick!

I haven't seen you at the University.

Are you a student?

Last semester. I stuck around for a few extra months. I've got cousins here.

I took a leave of absence to get my head in order. My mental health in the last couple years has not been... stellar.

I've been off kilter lately, too.

When I was a kid, I kept having this thought that the whole world could have suddenly begun existing in that moment...

...and that all my memories could have just been dreams.

And anyway, you never know what'll set you off. The human mind is unpredictable.

Yeah.

I've been trying to figure that out a bit more.

Dig into myself.

Sounds like a shit place to spend an evening. Better to smoke some more of my hash.

There's this one thing I keep going back to. A high school class.

You're determined to do this, huh? OK. Go ahead, make me your therapist.

What?

I'm serious. Go ahead.

I was sort of fucking up the class. Not doing the homework, talking back to the teacher.

Smart-ass.

Yeah.

So the teacher made me stay behind one day.

After everyone was gone, she made me lie facedown on the floor.

And then she told me to grind myself against the floor.

Sexual, but neither of us acknowledged it. And she just watched me. It was humiliating.

I can remember feeling my face flush hot as I stared down at the ground.

And then after a while she told me to stop and go home.

I didn't tell anybody obviously.

I got so angry at myself and I sort of turned inward and shut other people out.

There was this girl in that class that I liked. And I mean, really liked.

She was sarcastic. Really funny.

We joked all the time.

And she liked me back!

She didn't tell me outright, of course. It was high school. But she tried to hold my hand one day as we walked to the park after school.

I can still remember it so vividly, like a movie.

It was the day after the thing with the teacher.

And I just couldn't hold her hand back. I just let it slide off.

She never tried again.

It was like that with a few people.

What happened in the class?

Nothing. I got a shitty grade.

But I built this stupid shell around myself. It took years to break out.

And the whole thing just seems so weirdly fucking minor to have triggered that.

68

It's weird, but weird shit really happens. I'm sorry it happened to you.

Honestly, I wonder sometimes if it even happened or if I just made it up to justify being another sad-sack 21-year-old dude.

From personal observation, that seems to require very little justification.

Jesus. I'm sorry, I don't know why I just told you all of that.

We just met.

It's okay. It's nice you opened up to me.

Here, we can trade off. What's your worst story?

Worse than yours.

A shitty thing happened and it fucked me up. I'm not gonna write a book about it or anything.

I've been drawing comics again lately and it's coming out okay. Maybe I'll try to make a comic about that high school class.

A comic? You make comics?

I'm trying. We'll see.

...Can I buy more hash from you?

Sure. Just call it art supplies.

69

Meanwhile, Lebanon's crisis was becoming headline news back in the U.S. President Bush voiced his support for the anti-Syrian opposition, complicating the narrative of a popular uprising.

Today, America and Europe are standing together with the Lebanese people.

A Syrian withdrawal of all its military and intelligence personnel would help ensure that the Lebanese elections occur as scheduled in the spring, and that they will be free and fair.

The trend is clear: In the Middle East and throughout the world, freedom is on the march.

The movement, which had been called the "Intifada for Independence" was rebranded by American media as the "Cedar Revolution."

"Intifada" translates to "shaking off," but its association with the Palestinian uprisings was too much for CNN.

Pro-Syrian politicians raged at American meddling.

Tensions spread to campus.

Can you explain to me what the hell is going on here?

The prime minister resigned a week ago, and now he's back?

Well, a big part of it is sectarianism.

You have to be a Sunni Muslim to be the prime minister.

The president is always Maronite Christian.

PSSSH!

The speaker of parliament is always Shia.

It's super complicated, but it was the deal that ended the civil war.

And now that Hariri's dead, there's not a lot of Sunni politicians that the MPs can agree on.

But won't people just go back into the streets and drive him out again?

KNOCK
KNOCK

We're heading over to Sara's goodbye party. It's raining, so we're gonna take a taxi.

You're always out here, huh?

It is my apartment.

And I do smoke cigarettes.

Anyway, not for much longer.

This is Munir. He's a communist.

Munir, this is Andy.

He's a confused American sad sack.

Nice to meet you.

You too.

Sara, I can't believe you're leaving!

Yeah, no more therapy sessions.

NUDGE

I gotta go to the bathroom.

I can't. I'm sorry.

Just giving it a shot. Don't worry about it.

Anyway, I'm leaving, right?

Problem solved.

 I burned you that Nick Drake album.

Thanks.

 glug

 I hooked up with a guy for the first time last night.

Cool.

 It's been a weird day.

 I'm bi. I've had plenty of girlfriends. I'm not judging you.

Anyway, this is Beirut! Who gives a shit about stuff like that when we could have war again tomorrow?

 Was it nice?

 It was nice.

But I thought about my ex-girlfriend during a lot of it.

But it was nice.

 And then I thought about my ex-girlfriend all of today.

 It's such a stupid situation.

Whatever. Are you excited to be getting out of here?

Sort of, I guess. You can't say this place isn't interesting.

Tell me about this ex-girlfriend. I won't make fun of you this time.

It just worked somehow, like it never has with anyone else.

And she was pretty.

And she was pretty.

So why'd you break up?

Because I'm an idiot? I don't know.

I had an ex-girlfriend like that.

Here's a spoiler— It's probably not gonna get better.

So, fuck it, man. Let's go dance.

...

Yeah. Fuck it.

The struggle for Beirut's streets was far from over.

The opposition called for even bigger protests in Martyr's Square on March 14 to counter Hezbollah's rally the week before.

Campus that day was awash in the red, white and green of the Lebanese flag.

Sweating and shaking off a vicious hangover, I followed the streams of people toward downtown.

INDEPENDENCE 05

SY
OU
LE

The high school class I'd talked to Sara about the other night was on my mind.

There was more to it than what I'd told her.

85

Another student.

Popular, funny. At ease with himself in a way I wished I was.

Surprisingly, he wanted to be friends.

Then one day, in the middle of the semester while we were next to each other in the dark, watching another student present...

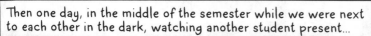

...he reached over and grabbed my crotch, while looking ahead and grinning.

I didn't want it. I didn't do anything.

I was ashamed.

After that that I stopped doing the classwork.

Which is when the teacher asked me to stay behind.

I turned a corner and was pulled back out into the present.

Fully a quarter of the country filled the streets of Beirut, the largest gathering in Lebanon's history.

Can I talk to you for a minute?

Sure, come in.

What happened two nights ago was really sweet.

I'm not expecting anything more.

I just don't want you to talk to Jason about what happened between us.

Is that cool?

I thought you said it was okay?

It is okay.

It's like an open relationship thing. But Jason doesn't want or need to know everything.

I just want you to know that he wouldn't be hurt if he knew, but it might be sort of weird.

And I want us all to stay friends.

All of us staying friends sounds pretty good.

Two days after the massive March 14 protest, as my political science class ended, students surrounded the professor and tried to talk him into running in the upcoming parliamentary elections.

They told him he was intelligent, charismatic, and outside the usual closely knit political dynasties.

He turned them down.

That night I had a nightmare of a man being beheaded outside my window.

I heard sounds from my kitchen and found it full of strangers who said they'd climbed through the windows, but not to worry, this building, and only this building, was safe.

I woke up in a sweat to the 5 a.m. call to prayer echoing through the city.

91

That morning, I bought a notebook from the stationery store near my apartment.

Back home, I began sketching out ideas for a comic about my high school class.

I spent the whole of Saturday planning out the project, working out the beats and themes.

In the evening, my friends came over for drinks and hash.

The triumphalism of the first protests was giving way to an unease that we all could feel.

93

"He lived up north, in the village my family's from."

"I didn't know him too well, really."

"How'd he die?"

"I dunno. Your parents don't tell you those things when you're a kid."

"Do you believe in ghosts?"

"Nope."

"Years after he died, at home in Boston, I was driving at night."

"And I saw him in the middle of the road in front of me."

"I was really tired. I might have been on mushrooms earlier."

"But I saw him there."

"What happened? Did he say anything to you?"

"He just looked at me as I drove through him and he disappeared."

94

The air of the city was thickening.

It was high time to get out of town for a few days.

RENTAL

Sami and Jason rented a car with another friend of theirs.

First we headed down to the South, to the white-sand beaches and Roman ruins of Tyre.

The next day we drove eastward to the mountains and forests of the Chouf.

Then we went to the north, up through the Kadisha Valley to the peaks of Mount Lebanon, still capped with snow and dotted with red-roofed villages hanging from the edges of cliffs.

CLICK!

We walked through cedar forests, taking their fresh scent deep into our lungs.

We chased a herd of goats down a hillside.

Then we drove down the valley to Sami's family village in the olive groves of the Koura district.

In his family's house, mostly empty since they moved to the States, we smoked hash and danced.

The next day we drove down to a hotel by the beach.

Sami's friend Amin had arranged a room there for his employer, a 54-year-old divorced, alcoholic Saudi tycoon.

We drank whiskey until our eyes crossed, and played cards.

Suddenly, the pop music videos on the hotel TV were interrupted by a news bulletin.

There had been another bombing.

BOOM

Six people were wounded. Nobody knew who'd done it.

Storms were rolling in from the sea as we drove back to Beirut the next morning.

I decided I needed to stop hooking up with Sami.

In my diary, I began to write of an unraveling, of scattering pieces of myself as I walked.

Paranoia clotted my thoughts whenever I was alone.

Kathy and I would exchange emails every few days.

Though filled with sadness, they were glimpses into a different, better lifetime.

On Friday, as I walked through campus, the air began swarming with tiny black insects.

Young ant queens and winged males were emerging from their nests in uncountable numbers, then swirling up into the heavens to mate, begin new colonies and die.

That night, a bomb went off in Broummana, wounding twelve.

BOOM

A well-dressed middle-aged man wandered through my neighborhood, crossing the street, doubling back on himself, and shouting "Today is the day!" in Arabic, until his voice was hoarse and cracking.

اليوم هو اليوم!

اليوم هو اليوم!

Pushed by the U.S., the UN Security Council authorized an investigation into Hariri's assassination.

Naïveté and the biggest army in the world is a dangerous combination.

That idea you have that you're this shining example is pretty deep.

People don't want to be like America, though. Everyone sees through your bullshit.

You just reelected George Bush for fuck's sake.

But they *do* want the stuff that America *has*.

Your movies, your burgers, your porn.

Munir, you're a communist, right?

Sure.

Does that mean you think a real revolution could actually come?

On a global scale.

But don't you think the systems would stop it? Just not let it happen?

The systems?!

Fuck the systems.

Are the systems working here?

Are the systems working anywhere?

flick

Oh no! She's caught a bug!

Aww. Who's my big hunter?

Tch! I wish she'd leave the poor thing alone.

My big, strong, insect killer!

Get him!

Look, she's just playing with it!

thwap!

Ok, habibti, that's enough. Let it go, sweetie. My big hunter....

MRRRRR

111

Still, I think the most important thing psychedelics did for me was teach me how fragile anyone's grip on reality really is.

Right, yeah. It's all so easy to alter.

Your vision, your perceptions of things.

We need to find more drugs, man.

Mina and I are working on it. You should come out tonight.

We've been meeting new people.

113

Whatever! Rootless!! That's the future, man!

Like this guy. He's half Lebanese, half Japanese. Talk about the future. Killer combo, huh?

I'm Daniel.

Nice to meet you, man. Living in a lot of places is good, you know. Broadens your horizons.

Fuck yeah, it does!

glug

You know, I even lived in Iran for a minute.

All you hear about Iran is oppressed women in veils and angry old dudes with beards.

But the craziest parties I have ever been to were in Iran.

You drive out of the city...

...it's nighttime...

...you're in the middle of nowhere...

...you come over a hill and boom, there's a giant fucking rave.

Fuck.

And every single person there is fucked up on ecstasy.

Every fucking person, man!

Tens of thousands of kids in a field, with lights and music and craziness and they're all fucked up out of their minds.

Hell of a lot more worth it than tens of thousands of kids out in Martyr's Square for the protests.

At least the ones at the rave get to have a good party.

I was just talking about missing drugs.

You ever do speed, man?

Too hard-core for you?

Fuck! No.

I'm telling you, man, speed is fun as shit.

You just can't fuck, is the one thing. Impossible to get a boner.

But you dance, you feel invincible, you wanna take on the world.

The other night I snorted some and I was near campus so I ran around the track, like, five times.

That was stupid, though. Think about your heart rate. You could have had a fucking heart attack.

True enough, man, true enough. But I had an awesome time doing it.

I felt like a fucking Olympian!

Unable to form a government, the prime minister resigned for the second time in three months, on the thirtieth anniversary of the outbreak of the civil war.

It was a holiday. Suleiman and I took a taxi downtown and wandered through crowds of people.

We passed rows of vendors hawking revolution kitsch.

Pop singers sang on a giant stage, their plastic faces illuminated by colored lights shining through fog machines.

Nice art.

My ex-girlfriend emailed me yesterday and told me she still misses me.

I think I really still love her.

Or least I want to love her.

But I can only imagine it somewhere else, sometime else.

Everything about me feels too fucked up right now to do it right.

Yeah. Maybe it's just being 21 years old, but a lot of things just fucking suck right now.

You know, I haven't actually had an orgasm from sex in like half a year.

119

Jesus. I'm sorry. That's fucked up.

It's okay. Sex is still fun.

But now it's just sort of frustrating at the end.

I don't know what changed.

I had an ex-girlfriend who never was able to cum.

The one who still misses you, who you're still basically in a relationship with but you won't admit it?

CLINK!

No. Different ex-girlfriend. Waaaay shittier ex-girlfriend.

But not because she wasn't able to cum! She was just kinda mean.

She wasn't even able to cum from masturbating?

Not even masturbating.

She told me months into our relationship.

I could tell she felt so terrible about it.

I remember the look on her face.

She was so sad.

120

 I felt super shitty that she'd felt she couldn't tell me for so long.

And of course I wanted to fix it....

 Of course.

 I actually bought this crazy thing off the internet for her.

You hook these pads up to your feet and drink a bunch of Gatorade...

 Gatorade?

 For the electrolytes?

 And then it's supposed to give you an orgasm easier.

 Huh. Did it work?

 I think so. It seemed like she had an orgasm.

But who knows, right?

I couldn't tell the difference before.

Anyway, we broke up almost immediately after.

Because you weren't sure if you could get her to cum or not?

No, because I realized she was an asshole.

I actually brought the orgasm thing here.

Pfft. Hahaha! Just in case?

Yeah, dude, just in case.

You can borrow it, if you don't think that's too weird.

Sure thing. I'll let you know.

We could use it now if you want.

What do you mean?

Everything sucks and is terrible and we're all going crazy.

We might as well fuck, right?

And you might as well get to orgasm.

We don't have to make anything of it.

gulp!

No need for attachment. Our sacred nihilism can remain intact.

Well, you sold yourself pretty hard with that story about not being able to get your ex-girlfriend to cum.

I'm finishing that wine bottle first.

123

I didn't cum.

Your orgasm machine fucking sucks.

I still feel like I'm going crazy.

Ha.

Go us.

I guess this shit's harder to shake than you'd think.

The international pressure over the string of bombings proved too much.

VRRROOOOOOOOOOOOOMM...

On April 26, Syria withdrew the last of its troops east across the border.

For the first time in 29 years, no foreign power occupied Lebanese soil.

Shit, man. I feel like hell.

We were up super late last night.

Uh. We've been doing speed.

Whoa. Dude. From Jamal and those guys?

Did you know he's a medical student?

I guess he got in trouble in the States and had to come here. And now he's training to be a doctor.

And the guns.

And he has these guns and he takes them out and shows them to us.

SNORT

And then there's his friend who was like, "I just finished a midterm, time to celebrate!" and this guy was just fucked up on heroin.

Lying on his couch.

But yes. We got it from Jamal.

126

127

Spring break came.

Sami, Mina, Lili, Suleiman and I took a trip to Jordan that was organized by the University.

The diary entry I recorded afterward is a list of bulleted sentences of scattered thoughts, ending with "write more later."

I never did.

The trip is a collection of scenes in my mind, a descent into the underworld.

VRRROOOOo

From the moment we got on the bus, I had the feeling of a dam bursting, water rushing through my body.

We swallowed pills that Daniel gifted us.

The Syrian border crossings were dreamy blurs.

In a Damascus suburb, Mina and Lili faked a panic attack and scored Valium at a pharmacy.

POP!

Jordan 2005 Pictures

In place of diary entries, I do have one record of the trip— 121 photographs that Sami shared with me.

It's strange, every single one of my own photos from my life that spring have vanished, lost to hard drive crashes, lapsed photo-sharing site accounts, and the passage of 13 years.

But the images from this trip, taken by another, have stayed with me.

We look so young in them.

129

We drove in 4x4s into Wadi Rum, the vast red desert in the south of Jordan.

Around us, the striated earth soared to dizzying heights.

We ran down sand dunes.

oof!

We slept in canvas tents.

We ate chicken under a thousand stars.

A million stars. A billion stars.

Everything was beautiful, even the darkness we all could see at the edges.

We went to Petra, the crumbling capital of the ancient Nabateans.

All around us, monumental façades gave the appearance of rose-colored palaces, but in fact were the entryways to tombs.

SNRT

Lili and I found a small, hidden place and snorted the last of the speed.

The stone city jolted to life.

Astonished and sweating in the hot sun, we wandered through its decorated valleys.

1,300 years of rain and wind had worn some sandstone tombs down like melted candles.

Others stood proud, almost untouched by the centuries.

The air vibrated.

Heat waves rose from the sandy floor.

I climbed a staircase hidden in the rocks. Two goats stared at me.

My face felt flushed and red as I crested and the ancient city spread out before me.

One night in a hotel room—I think it was the last of the trip, but I can't be sure—Sami, Lili, Mina and I divvied up the remaining Valium tablets.

I half remember bits of conversation...

...that gradually shift into me kissing Lili first...

...then Sami...

...then Sami kissing Mina as Lili and I undressed.

Different hands ran across my body as my hands ran across different bodies.

We kissed each other hazily.

No further, I think.

A knock at the door, and everyone stopped kissing each other. The fog clears a bit from my memory.

KNOCK
KNOCK

It was Suleiman.

He said he'd been hiding Valium pills in his underwear. Sad or angry that he'd been left out of the hotel room, he'd swallowed all of them at once.

He grinned his crooked smile at me, then collapsed.

Slowed by the drugs, I didn't catch him.

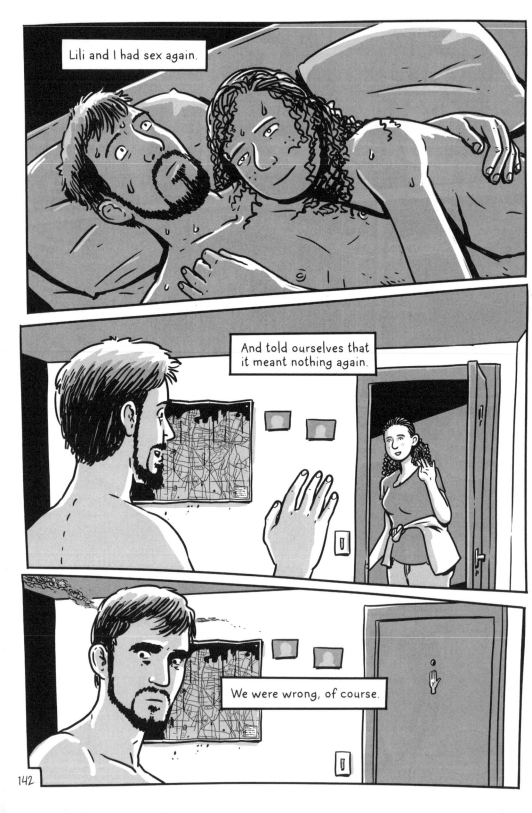

The next day, I was working on the comic about the high school class.

It had grown strange.

I'd begun to structure it around a sort of performance in which my present self was forced to view my past self, then strangle it.

A shudder passed through me. The hair on my arms stood up.

Something had been waiting, just off-stage, watching me.

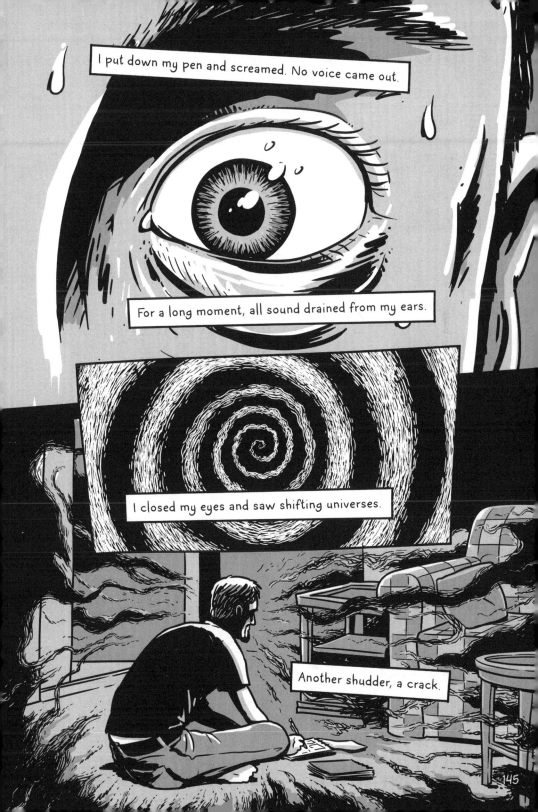

I walked to the internet café, trying to clear my head.

An email from Kathy, sad at how much of a wall had come up between us.

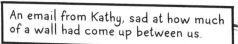

Another shudder.

149

My skin crawled.

I opened the window.

A breeze blew against the curtains.

Cool air tinted with salt, up from the sea.

I crawled out on the air-conditioning unit, nine floors above the street.

And sat there.

As night was finally falling, my phone rang.

BZZZZZ

It was Lili.

They'd been at Jamal's apartment, high on speed for a day and a half, and had bought a ball of hash the size of a softball for me.

153

Here.

Thanks.

You're a fucking asshole.

I know. I'm sorry.

I don't even know why I got this for you.

You know I haven't actually even slept since you tried to pawn me off on that fucking guy at your party?

Like it was your right?

Like, listen, I know we said we weren't going to get attached.

And maybe I got attached despite myself.

But that doesn't give you any fucking right to try to set me up with someone else the night after we fuck.

Can you *imagine* how insulting that was?

You're right. I was an idiot. There's no excuse for it.

I think I just almost killed myself.

Really? *Fucking really?*

Are you trying to make me feel sorry for you now?

That's so goddamn manipulative, you shit.

Can you not even take responsibility for your own fucking actions?

I wish I could take all that stuff back.

I wish I could just take everything back.

Well, you can't.

You don't get a rewrite on stuff like this.

But you know what?

I don't even think I'm that pissed at you.

I'm angry at myself.

I'm angry that I got hurt from this because it's so stupid.

You mooning over your ex-girlfriend, fucking whatever comes your way.

I should have seen it coming.

Is it this fucking city?

Can I talk to you in the back room?

Sure. What's up?

I'm going to get Mina. I'll be right back.

So what's up?

My mother takes pills for anxiety.

I've been stealing them from her.

One at a time.

I've got a lot.

Suleiman, what are you going to do?

I'm going to take them all tomorrow and kill myself.

WHAT?

I can't do this anymore. They hate me. I hate me.

I'm tired.

Suleiman, you can't.

You can't!

I've tried to do it three times before.

But it didn't work.

This time I've got enough, I think.

Promise me you won't.

You can move out of your parents' house!

You'll get a boyfriend. You can move in with him.

Just promise us.

Please.

Not tomorrow.

...Not tomorrow.

Not tomorrow.

What's wrong?

Another bomb exploded. In Jounieh.

BOOM

They don't know if anyone died yet.

161

One by one, the young men left in the protest tent encampments drifted away.

The streets, two months earlier a river of people with the future shining from their eyes, were filled with taxi drivers and shopping families.

I wrote final papers for my classes.

I hung out and talked with Lili.

I watched movies with Sami.

No point in feigning surprise

And I drew.

I drew and I drew and I drew.

When I wasn't drawing, I was writing ideas for stories to draw.

Something had come unstoppered in me.

My brother visited from New York.

With Sami, we rented a car and traveled the length and breadth of the country.

From the border walls and crusader castles of the south to the markets of Tripoli and olive orchards of the north.

From the beaches of the coast up through the mountain gorges to the roman temples of the Bekaa Valley.

We drank absinthe, took boat rides through flooded caves, danced at house parties, danced at clubs.

Then he was gone.

BEEP!

TAXI

Elections came and the streets were filled again by cars with blaring loudspeakers.

BEEP!! BEEP!

صوتوا!

Beirut seemed tired. Worn-out.

BEEP! BEEP!

BEEP!

BEEEEP!!

My last weeks in the country sped by.

My diary entries become far fewer and are filled with loneliness, but my handwriting evens out again in them.

Suleiman didn't take the pills he stole from his mother.

I didn't sleep with Sami or Lili again.

We all stayed friends.

I don't remember this time clearly. Who I talked to, or where I went.

The week before I left I took a trip to Syria.

I can picture it vividly in my mind, but when I went to look for it in my diary, it was omitted completely.

It was me, Sami, Jason, our across-the-street-neighbor Elisa, and her sister.

The five of us took a taxi all the way from Beirut to Damascus.

We spent a day and a night in the bustling Syrian capital.

Then we booked cabins on the night train north to Aleppo.

We took the night train back from Aleppo to Damascus.

Sami and Jason shared a cabin.

Elisa and her sister shared one, too.

As the odd one out, my cabin-mate was an old man—a stranger.

gurgle

Something—maybe the sausage—didn't sit well.

plop

I spent the night in the toilet.

HURK

169

I finished up my finals.

Thank you & have a grea

BOOM

An anti-Syrian journalist was killed in a car bomb.

I said goodbye to my friends.

I'd been in Beirut for five months.

A lifetime.

Not even half a year.

170

Beirut was the same, Beirut was different.

The city had another war notched on its belt.

In July of 2006, Israeli warplanes pounded Lebanon for 18 days, killing over a thousand Lebanese civilians and smashing bridges, water treatment plants and power stations.

BOOM

No matter. More glimmering skyscrapers had sprouted along the shores of the Mediterranean.

I was the same, I was different.

The instability inside me had ebbed.

We'd come to Beirut again for Kathy's job, and while we were there, I worked as a guest editor on a Lebanese comics magazine called *Samandal*.

We became good friends with the editors.

...then you lay down the ink.

Beirut opened itself up to us.

It was wonderful, a completely different city than I'd known by myself.

One hot night in the summer, toward the end of our stay, we were out dancing with friends.

glug!

Through the crowd, I saw a face I knew.

Suleiman!

...Andy?!

How are you?

I'm good, man!

177

I'd flown into Rafik Hariri International Airport.

A billboard in front of my neighborhood with his smiling face read "truth for the sake of Lebanon."

الحقيقة لأجل لبنان

Silver footprints in the Place d'Etoiles, marked his last steps as he walked toward his motorcade.

His statue by Rue Minet al-Hosn gazed serenely at the bend in the road where his body lay dying.

I started research for a comic about him, trying to come to grips with the events of 2005.

The more I dug, the more contradictions I found.

He built hospitals and schools for the poor and the victims of conflict in the middle of Lebanon's fifteen year war.

He also gobbled up miles of real estate to create a soulless playground for rich tourists, made off with billions, and left his country drowning in debt.

Pro-Syrian, then anti-Syrian, then dead. I couldn't get a handle on him.

Samir Kassir. Journalist and founder of the Democratic Left Movement. Kill... car bomb, 6/2/...

George Hawi. Former leader of the Lebanese Communist Party. Killed 6/21/2005.

Elias Murr. Defense Minister, son-in-law of President Lahoud. Wounded by car bomb, 6/12/2005.

The assassination of Rafik Hariri was never solved.

May Chidiac. Journalist. Wounded by car bomb, 9/25/2005. Arm and leg amputated.

Gebran Tueni. Journalist and Member of Parliament. Killed by...

Pierre Amine Gemayel. Member of Parliament. Shot to death, 11/21/2006.

The UN Special Tribunal released arrest warrants for four suspects, all Hezbollah members, but the suspects vanished.

Walid Eido. Member of Parliament. Killed by car bomb, 6/...

Antoine Ghanem. Member of Parliament.

Francois Elias Hajj. Brigadier General. ...ed by car bomb, ...2/2007.

The perpetrators of the random bombings were never found either, their motives never uncovered.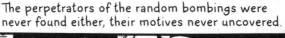

Wissam Eid. Investigator into the assassination of Rafik Hariri. Killed by car bomb, 1/25/2008.

Saleh Aridi, Lebanese Democratic Party politician. Killed by car bo...

Kamal Naji. Deputy representative of the PLO in Lebanon. Killed ...bomb,

Since 1976, no political assassination in Lebanon has truly been solved.

General Wissam al-Hassan. Head of Internal Security Forces' Information Branch. Killed by car bomb, 10/19/2012.

Mohamad Chatah. Former Finance Minister. Killed by car bomb, 12/27/2012.

Bodies upon bodies upon bodies.

The Occupy Wall Street movement was on television screens as I returned to the States that September.

WALL STREET PROTEST GROWING FAST
Group says it's protesting "corporate greed"

A shaking off.

WE ARE THE 99%

OCCUPY WALL STREET

WE ARE THE 99%!

It was broken and scattered by the time fall turned to winter.

I wrote the comic about the assassination of Rafik Hariri, but I left out my own crisis.

It gnawed at me.

183

The Lebanese government deadlocked, crumbled, reformed, and deadlocked again.

Alliances changed, the politicians remained the same.

Next door, the Syrian uprising turned into the Syrian civil war.

ISIS, a nightmare born in the rubble of the U.S. invasion of Iraq, fed off the chaos, and thrived.

I cried when I saw the photos of Aleppo's markets burning.

I cried when I watched the videos of the bodies in the Mediterranean.

Crying didn't stop it.

As for me, I never came undone again like that day in Beirut in 2005, but there were moments that shook me.

Once, at the tail end of a mushroom trip, an enormous blue eye appeared to me, staring into my depths.

Another time, at a concert in San Francisco, black clouded my vision. I groped my way to the bar, blind and sweating.

There are small things, too. I mutter. I'm not kind to myself when I am alone.

BZZZZZZZZ

SWEEP SWEEP

But time kept passing, and things stayed put together.

I kept circling back to Beirut.

Aleppo, the largest and oldest city in Syria

In 2015, I made another comic about 2005, this time about my trip to Syria with Sami and Jason.

Again, I carefully left out the breakdown.

Working on it, I remembered the odd conviction I'd had back then that I was a character in my own book. It felt like an unpaid debt to a self long gone, but part of me.

So, 14 years later, I tried for a third time, and began work on this book.

That December, my mom and I went walking near my parents' home in California.

Gunmetal waves lapped at the beach.

Gray rocks speckled with anemones.

Hermit crabs.

The tide was coming in.

I wanted her blessing to write about my grandmother and aunt. For the first time, I told her about the breakdown.

The manic episode.

Whatever it was.

What I saw then, what I heard, what I felt— I couldn't distinguish what was real and what wasn't.

I think it brought me back to making comics, but it also feels like it's a glimpse of something that could happen again.

You know, even when I knew I was almost certainly old enough to be beyond it, it was always in the back of my mind.

That maybe it would happen to me.

Maybe it would happen to one of you.

But I've also always found that fear kind of drives me.

To try things. To get done as much as I can, before it gets me.

★ ROSAMUNDE

I had dinner with Mina in the spring and told her I was writing this book.

It's interesting to me that you went back.

It had been ten years since I'd seen her.

I never did. My feelings about Beirut are still so wrapped up in our time then.

Our memories sometimes matched, sometimes differed, two paintings of the same landscape by different artists.

It was quite hard.

I think we were all so sad.

And I was so self-destructive then.

I remember the feeling that I couldn't connect with anyone.

She asked that her name be changed, so I did so.

She hadn't spoken with Lili in six years.

I was in the city for a week, a guest at a conference and gala for a comics award that I'd helped judge the year before.

Let's hear it for... comics!!!

The award was funded by a wealthy businessman and the gala was strange, a mix of high society and scrappy cartoonists.

The city was quiet.

So now the giant robot's kind of a hermit.

Hmm...

There had been protests a year and a half before, over botched trash collection, but the movement had died down.

Refugee children from the Syrian civil war sold roses to Beirutis drinking beer at outdoor bars.

Not long before I left again, I wandered around my old neighborhood, looking for the building where I'd lived in 2005.

I wanted to take pictures of it I could draw from.

I got lost.

There were huge modern apartment blocks in unfamiliar places.

For a minute, I thought I couldn't find it.

I thought it was gone, torn down to make room for new development.

I saw the dogs first.

ACKNOWLEDGMENTS

Thanks to Mom, Dad, Toby and Livy for being the wonderful, complicated people whom I have the privilege of calling my family. Showing this to you was terrifying, and your support made me feel so loved.

Thanks to fdz, Omar, Hatem, Lena, Joseph and everyone associated with *Samandal* throughout the years for your friendship and for being the first people anywhere to believe in me enough to publish my comics. Thanks to Leila and Chris for being great friends and housemates during Kathy and my stay in Beirut in 2011. Thanks to Lina and JAD for bringing me out to Beirut in 2016 and 2017 and for your limitless hospitality once I was there. Thanks to all my friends from Lebanon in 2005, those who ended up in this book, and those who didn't. I think of you often, and I hope I've done okay by your stories.

Thanks to Shawkat, Deborah, Munther and the Cornell University Near Eastern Studies Department for the education and encouragement when I was so young.

Thanks to Dakota and dw for reading drafts. Thanks to fdz for being honest enough to tell me when I've fucked something up, for correcting my crappy Arabic, and for putting me up when I come to town. Thanks to my editor, Anna DeVries, for seeing something in my comics years ago, and sticking by me. Thanks to my agent, Farley Chase, for fighting to give me a chance to tell the stories I felt I needed to tell.

While working on this book I received a Civic Arts Grant for Individual Artists from the City of Berkeley, and I am deeply grateful for their support.

Thanks to Lisa, Steve and Teemu for making our compund a home. Thanks to Will and Ollie for giving me a light I didn't know I lacked. Most of all thanks to Kathy for sticking around and sharing her life with me.

APPENDIX A: MAPS

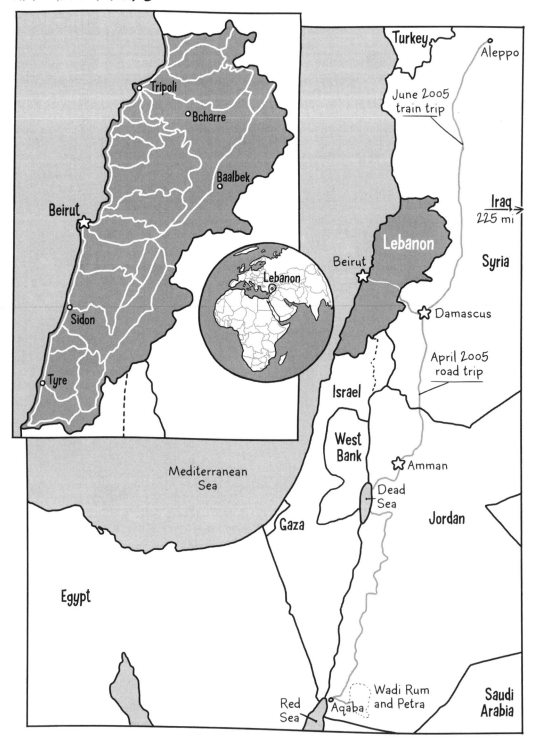

APPENDIX B: POLITICAL TIMELINE of LEBANON

Control of Lebanon and Syria passes from Ottoman Empire to French colonial adminstrators in the aftermath of World War I. — 1920

Lebanon achieves independence under a system of mandated power sharing between sects. — 1944

The creation of the state of Israel propels a wave of Palestinian refugees fleeing into Lebanon. — 1948

Civil war briefly breaks out over conflict between Pan-Arabism and Lebanese Nationalism. U.S.A. sends troops to Beirut to prop up government. — 1958

Israel launches airstrikes on Beirut's airport. — 1968

Palestinian Liberation Organization (PLO) moves headquarters to Beirut. — 1970

Lebanese civil war breaks out as violent reprisals between Palestinians and Christian militias expands into broader sectarian and political conflict. — 1975

Syria sends troops to Lebanon in support of the government. — 1976

Israel sends troops to Lebanon to attack PLO, sets up Christian puppet government (SLA) in south Lebanon. — 1978

Israel launches broad invasion of Lebanon, pushing Syrian army and PLO out of Beirut and seizing the west of the capital. Lebanese president assassinated, setting off bloody reprisal attacks against Palestinian civilians in Sabra and Shatila refugee camps. Multinational forces, including U.S. Marines, sent to support Lebanese government. — 1982

Lebanese government collapses, multinational forces withdraw after deadly suicide bombings. Sectarian and political violence intensifies. — 1983 -1989

Ta'if accords officially end hostilities in Lebanese civil war, all militias except Hezbollah and SLA disarm. — 1990

Lebanese Civil War

First Lebanese elections since 1972. Rafik Hariri becomes prime minister. — 1992

Israel bombs Lebanon, targeting Hezbollah bases. — 1996

SLA collapses, Israel withdraws from south Lebanon. Rafik Hariri becomes prime minister a second time. — 2000

U.S. invasion of Iraq increases regional instability. — 2003

Assassination of Rafik Hariri prompts widespread street protests, collapse of Lebanese government, and eventual withdrawal of Syrian forces from Lebanon. — 2005

Israel launches airstrikes on Lebanon after Hezbollah kidnaps Israeli soldiers. — 2006

Clashes break out between supporters of Hezbollah and Lebanese government. — 2008

Uprisings spread across Arab world. Syrian protests escalate into civil war. — 2011

Hezbollah intervenes in Syrian civil war in support of Syrian government. Worsening violence propels a wave of Syrian refugees fleeing into Lebanon. — 2013

Lebanon experiences bouts of sectarian fighting, militia battles and bombings as spillover from Syrian civil war. Refugee crisis intesifies dramatically. — 2013 -2017

Syrian Civil War

CHIK
CHIK
CHIK